Christmas COOKIES

Christmas COOKIES

Festive treats to bake and eat

Introduction by Linda Doeser
New recipes written by Sandra Baddeley
Cover design by Donna-Marie Scrase and Talking Design
Design by Donna-Marie Scrase
Additional and cover photography by Clive Streeter
Additional food styling by Angela Drake

Notes for the Reader
This book uses imperial, metric, and US cup measurements. Follow the same units of measurement throughout; do not mix imperial and metric. All spoon measurements are level: teaspoons are assumed to be 5 ml, and tablespoons are assumed to be 15 ml. Unless otherwise stated, milk is assumed to be whole, eggs are large, individual vegetables, such as potatoes, are medium, and pepper is freshly ground black pepper.

The times given are an approximate guide only. Preparation times differ according to the techniques used by different people and the cooking times may also vary from those given as a result of the type of oven used. Optional ingredients, variations or serving suggestions have not been included in the calculations.

Recipes using raw or very lightly cooked eggs should be avoided by infants, the elderly, pregnant women, convalescents, and anyone with a chronic condition. Pregnant and breastfeeding women are advised to avoid eating peanuts and peanut products. People with nut allergies should be aware that some of the ready-prepared ingredients used in the recipes in this book may contain nuts. Always check the packaging before use.

CONTENTS

INTRODUCTION

For centuries delicious edible treats have been as integral to traditional Christmas celebrations as a kiss beneath the mistletoe. In the week leading up to the great day generations have rolled up their sleeves and bustled about their kitchens baking—cakes particularly, but also breads, pastries, and cookies.

Every country has its own culinary traditions. In France, for example, village children would go from house to house singing carols on Christmas Eve and were rewarded with cornmeal wafers, while warmer spices featured in the cookies from further north— Dutch *speculaas*, German *lebkuchen*, Swedish *papparkakor*, and British gingerbread men.

However, it is in the United States where the tradition of baking Christmas cookies has grown and flourished. European immigrants took their Christmas recipes across the Atlantic with them and a new seasonal custom took root. Starting with the invention of the sugar cookie in Pennsylvania, American cooks have developed a vast array of tasty Christmas treats to give as gifts, to offer visiting friends, family, and neighbors, to hang on the Christmas tree, and, of course, to accompany a glass of milk left out for Santa on Christmas Eve.

A SEASONAL TOUCH

Cookies with a Christmas theme are easy to make and decorate. If you make a dough that can be rolled out, you can cut out any number of seasonal shapes. A huge range of specially shaped cookie cutters is available—holly leaves, snowflakes, stars, bells, Christmas trees, reindeer, Santa (with or without his sleigh or sack), Christmas stockings, angels, and candy canes, among others. These will always be popular with children and make lovely edible decorations. However, cookies made by the whisking method taste equally delicious and, even if they're a less fancy shape, can be decorated just as attractively.

You don't have to be particularly artistic to decorate Christmas-themed cookies, just in a festive frame of mind. In fact, it's a wonderful pre-Christmas activity to share with excited children and even preschoolers can drizzle frosting and sprinkle colored sugar with a surprising degree of accuracy.

A simple glace icing, made with confectioners' sugar and lemon juice or hot water flavored with vanilla extract, or a frosting glaze, made with confectioners' sugar, lemon juice, and egg white, are ideal for drizzling, piping, or spreading on cookies. Both are easily colored with a few drops of food coloring.

Once the cookies are frosted, a good supply of colored and chocolate sprinkles, gold and silver balls, sugar shapes, such as stars and flowers, edible glitter, and even small candies can be applied immediately and will keep children happily, if slightly messily, occupied for half an hour. Almost as easy is to decorate with colored sugar. Mix superfine sugar with a little food coloring paste in a polythene bag, rubbing it well in, then sprinkle over unset frosting or a topping of melted chocolate.

Piped frosting decorations always look special but do take a little practice and a fairly steady hand. Cookies are a good place to begin as they are small, easy to handle, and a homemade quality only adds to their charm. Food-coloring pens can sometimes be a good alternative to piping. Available in a wide range of colors, these look like felt-tip pens and can be used to decorate dry, firm frosting. They are ideal for writing names, initials, and messages on cookies, drawing designs such as stripes, spots, and stars, and for coloring in shapes.

WE WISH YOU A MERRY CHRISTMAS

Frosted cookies make delightful Christmas tree decorations. Before baking, use a skewer or knitting needle to pierce a hole in the top of each cookie that will be large enough to thread ribbon through. You may need to pierce again after cooking as the dough spreads during baking and may partially close the holes. Spread the cookies with frosting, decorate, and let set before threading thin ribbon through the holes, knotting, and hanging from the tree.

Cookies with a jeweled or stained glass effect also look lovely hanging from the Christmas tree. You can make these any shape you like. For example, stamp out stars from a rolled-out cookie dough, then stamp out smaller stars or rounds

from the centers, leaving a frame all around. Don't forget to pierce holes in the tops for hanging. Bake the cookies on a lined cookie sheet for about 5 minutes in a preheated oven, 350°F/180°C, for about 5 minutes, then remove from the oven, and fill the centers of each with crushed hard candy (don't mix the colors in the same cookie). Return to the oven and bake for another 5–8 minutes, until the cookies are golden and the candies have melted and filled the spaces. Let cool until the centers have set, then carefully remove from the cookie sheet. There are several recipes for these popular edible decorations in this book.

Homemade cookies make a thoughtful gift, especially for the elderly or those who live a long way from their families. Spending your time and effort baking cookies makes the gift seem particularly precious, especially in our busy modern age. To make them even more special wrap them prettily. An easy way is to cut a square of cellophane, make a pile of cookies in the center, gather up the edges, and tie the cellophane together with a ribbon or piece of wraphia. Packing the cookies in an attractive storage jar makes a two-in-one present and will also keep the cookies fresh. Similarly, you could pack cellophane-wrapped cookies inside a cup standing on a saucer ready for morning coffee on Christmas Day.

A final touch would be to make an edible gift tag. Roll out cookie dough and cut out a Christmas shape, such as a Christmas tree, holly leaf, or bell, using a small cookie cutter. Make a hole in the top with a skewer or knitting needle large enough to thread ribbon through and bake. When cool, coat with frosting, decorate, and write your message, then thread with ribbon and tie on your gift.

Snowflake
GINGERBREAD

Makes 30

- 3 cups all-purpose flour, plus extra for dusting
- 1 tbsp ground ginger
- 1 tsp baking soda
- scant ½ cup butter, softened, plus extra for greasing
- heaping ¾ cup brown sugar
- 1 egg, beaten
- 4 tbsp light corn syrup

To decorate

- 1 cup confectioners' sugar
- 2 tbsp lemon juice

1 Preheat the oven to 350°F/180°C. Grease three cookie sheets.

2 Sift the flour, ginger, and baking soda together into a bowl. Add the butter and rub into the flour until the mixture resembles fine breadcrumbs, then stir in the brown sugar.

3 In another bowl, beat together the egg and light corn syrup with a fork. Pour this mixture into the flour mixture and mix to make a smooth dough, kneading lightly with your hands.

4 Roll the dough out on a lightly floured surface to about ¼ inch/5 mm thick and cut into shapes using a snowflake-shape cutter. Transfer the cookies to the prepared cookie sheets.

5 Bake in the preheated oven for 10 minutes, until golden brown. Let cool for 5 minutes before transferring, using a spatula, to a wire rack to cool completely.

6 Once the cookies are cool, combine the confectioners' sugar and lemon juice until smooth and spoon into a pastry bag fitted with a very small tip. Pipe snowflake shapes onto each cookie with the icing. Let set for a few hours.

Eggnog
COKIES

Makes 35

- 1 egg
- heaping ¾ cup superfine sugar
- 6 tbsp rum
- 3 tbsp milk
- ½ cup butter, softened, plus extra for greasing
- 1 tsp vanilla extract
- 2 egg yolks
- 2½ cups all-purpose flour
- 1 tsp baking powder
- ¾ tsp ground nutmeg
- 1½ cups confectioners' sugar

1 Preheat the oven to 325°F/160°C. Grease two cookie sheets. To make the eggnog mixture, beat together the egg, 2 tablespoons of the superfine sugar, the rum, and milk until frothy. Set aside.

2 In a large bowl, beat together the rest of the superfine sugar and all but 1 tablespoon of the butter until light and fluffy. Beat in the vanilla extract and egg yolks until smooth.

3 Sift together the flour, baking powder, and ½ teaspoon of the nutmeg into the mixture and beat in ½ cup of the eggnog mixture until just combined.

4 Place heaping teaspoonfuls of the mixture on the prepared cookie sheets, spaced well apart. Flatten slightly with damp fingers and bake in the preheated oven for 20–25 minutes, or until the bottoms of the cookies turn golden.

5 Let cool for 5 minutes on the cookie sheets and then transfer to a wire rack to cool completely.

6 Once the cookies are cool, beat together the confectioners' sugar, remaining butter, and the remaining eggnog mixture to make a soft frosting.

7 Spread the frosting over the cookies and sprinkle with a little nutmeg on top. Let set for a few hours.

13

Spiced
RUM COOKIES

Makes 18

- ¾ cup unsalted butter, plus extra for greasing
- 1 cup dark brown sugar
- 2 cups all-purpose flour
- pinch of salt
- ½ tsp baking soda
- 1 tsp ground cinnamon
- ½ tsp ground coriander
- ½ tsp ground nutmeg
- ¼ tsp ground cloves
- 2 tbsp dark rum

1 Preheat the oven to 350°F/180°C. Grease two cookie sheets.

2 Cream together the butter and sugar and whisk until light and fluffy. Sift the flour, salt, baking soda, cinnamon, coriander, nutmeg, and cloves into the creamed mixture.

3 Pour the dark rum into the creamed mixture and stir well. Using 2 teaspoons, place small mounds of the mixture onto the prepared cookie sheets. Flatten each one slightly with the back of a spoon.

4 Bake in the preheated oven for 10–12 minutes, or until golden. Let the cookies cool and become crisp on wire racks before serving.

CHECKERBOARDS

Makes about 20

- 1 cup butter, softened
- ¾ cup superfine sugar
- 1 egg, separated and lightly beaten
- 2 tsp vanilla extract
- 2 cups all-purpose flour
- pinch of salt
- 1 tsp ground ginger
- 1 tbsp finely grated orange rind
- 1 tbsp unsweetened cocoa

1 Place the butter and sugar in a large bowl and beat together until light and fluffy, then beat in the egg yolk and vanilla extract. Sift together the flour and salt into the mixture and stir until combined.

2 Divide the dough in half. Add the ginger and orange rind to one half and mix well. Shape the dough into a log 6 inches/15 cm long. Flatten the sides and top to square off the log to 2 inches/5 cm high. Wrap in plastic wrap and chill in the refrigerator for 30–60 minutes.

3 Sift the cocoa into the other half of the dough and mix well. Shape into a flattened log exactly the same size as the first one, wrap in plastic wrap, and chill in the refrigerator for 30–60 minutes.

4 Unwrap the two doughs and cut each log lengthwise into three slices. Cut each slice lengthwise into three strips. Brush the strips with egg white and stack them in threes, alternating the colors, so they are the same shape as the original logs. Wrap in plastic wrap and chill for 30–60 minutes.

5 Preheat the oven to 375°F/ 190°C. Line two large cookie sheets with parchment paper.

6 Unwrap the logs and cut into slices with a sharp serrated knife, then place the cookies on the prepared cookie sheets, spaced well apart. Bake in the preheated oven for 12–15 minutes, or until firm. Let cool for 5–10 minutes, then transfer the cookies to wire racks to cool completely.

Santa
SUGAR COOKIES

Makes 40

- 3 cups all-purpose flour, plus extra for dusting
- 1 tsp baking powder
- ¼ tsp salt
- ½ cup butter, softened, plus extra for greasing
- heaping ¾ cup superfine sugar
- 1 egg, beaten
- 2½ tsp vanilla extract
- 1 tbsp milk

To decorate
- 2 cups confectioners' sugar
- 1 egg white
- ½ tsp glycerin
- glycerin-based red and black food coloring

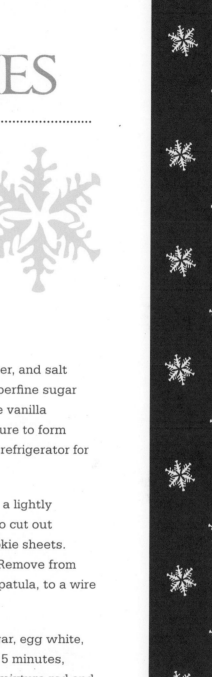

1 Grease four cookie sheets. Sift together the flour, baking powder, and salt together into a bowl. In a separate bowl, beat the butter and superfine sugar together until light and fluffy. Beat in the egg, 2 teaspoons of the vanilla extract, and the milk until smooth and then mix in the flour mixture to form a soft dough. Cover the dough with plastic wrap and chill in the refrigerator for 30 minutes.

2 Preheat the oven to 350°F/180°C. Roll out the chilled dough on a lightly floured surface to ¼ inch/5 mm thick. Use a Santa-shape cutter to cut out shapes from the dough. Transfer the cookies to the prepared cookie sheets. Bake in the preheated oven for 10 minutes, until golden brown. Remove from the oven and let cool for 5 minutes before transferring, using a spatula, to a wire rack to cool completely.

3 Once the cookies are cool, beat together the confectioners' sugar, egg white, remaining vanilla extract, and glycerin with an electric mixer for 5 minutes, until stiff and glossy. Color one-third of the confectioners' sugar mixture red and color 2 tablespoons of the mixture black. Leave the rest of the mixture as white icing. Apply the red icing evenly with a small spatula to create Santa's hat, and pipe eyes in black icing using a fine nozzle. Put the white icing into a pastry bag fitted with a small star-shaped tip to create the fur cuff, eyebrows, moustache, and bobble on Santa's hat. Apply the remainder of the icing, using a swirling action, with a small spatula to create his beard. Let set for a few hours.

19

Reindeer
COOKIES

Makes 25

- 10 cardamom pods
- scant ½ cup butter, softened, plus extra for greasing
- ¼ cup superfine sugar
- 1 egg, beaten
- finely grated rind of ½ orange
- 2 cups all-purpose flour, plus extra for dusting
- ¼ cup cornstarch
- ½ tsp baking powder

To decorate

- heaping ¾ cup confectioners' sugar
- 4 tsp lemon juice
- glycerin-based red food coloring
- 25 edible silver balls

1 Crush the cardamom pods lightly in a pestle with a mortar and discard the shells. Grind the cardamom seeds to a powder. Beat together the butter and superfine sugar in a bowl with a whisk until creamy, then gradually beat in the egg, orange rind, and cardamom powder.

2 Sift together the flour, cornstarch, and baking powder into the mixture and stir with a wooden spoon to form a soft dough. Wrap the dough in plastic wrap and chill in the refrigerator for 30 minutes.

3 Preheat the oven to 350°F/180°C. Grease three cookie sheets. Roll out the chilled dough on a lightly floured surface to ⅛ inch/3 mm thick. Cut out shapes using a reindeer-shape cutter and place on the prepared cookie sheets. Reknead and reroll the trimmings and cut out more shapes until all the dough is used up.

4 Bake in the preheated oven for 15 minutes, until just golden. Let cool for 5 minutes before transferring, using a spatula, to a wire rack to cool completely. Combine the confectioners' sugar and lemon juice until smooth. Spoon 2 tablespoons of the mixture into a separate mixing bowl and color it with the red food coloring.

5 Spoon the rest of the icing into a pastry bag fitted with a fine tip and pipe antlers, hoofs, tail, collar, and a saddle in white icing on each cookie. Pipe a nose using the red icing. For the eye, attach a silver ball using a blob of icing.

Sugar
COOKIE HEARTS

Makes about 30

- 1 cup butter, softened
- 1½ cups superfine sugar
- 1 egg yolk, lightly beaten
- 2 tsp vanilla extract
- heaping 1¾ cups all-purpose flour
- ¼ cup unsweetened cocoa
- pinch of salt
- 3–4 food coloring pastes
- 3½ oz/100 g semisweet chocolate, broken into pieces

1 Place the butter and half of the sugar in a large bowl and beat together until light and fluffy, then beat in the egg yolk and vanilla extract. Sift together the flour, cocoa, and salt into the mixture and stir until combined. Halve the dough, shape into balls, wrap in plastic wrap, and chill for 30–60 minutes.

2 Preheat the oven to 375°F/190°C. Line two large cookie sheets with parchment paper. Unwrap the dough and roll out between two sheets of parchment paper. Cut out cookies with a heart-shape cutter and place them on the prepared cookie sheets, spaced well apart. Bake in the preheated oven for 10–15 minutes, or until firm. Let cool on the cookie sheets for 5–10 minutes, then transfer to wire racks to cool completely.

3 Meanwhile, divide the remaining sugar among four small plastic bags or bowls. Add a little food coloring paste to each and rub in until well mixed. Wear a plastic glove if mixing in bowls to prevent your hands from getting stained. Place the chocolate in a heatproof bowl, set the bowl over a saucepan of gently simmering water, and heat until melted. Let cool slightly.

4 Leave the cookies on the racks. Spread the melted chocolate over them and sprinkle with the colored sugar. Let set.

Cinnamon & Chocolate
CHIP COOKIES

Makes about 30

- 1 cup butter, softened
- scant ¾ cup superfine sugar
- 1 egg yolk, lightly beaten
- 2 tsp orange extract
- 2½ cups all-purpose flour
- pinch of salt
- heaping ½ cup semisweet chocolate chips

Cinnamon coating
- 1½ tbsp superfine sugar
- 1½ tbsp ground cinnamon

1 Preheat the oven to 375°F/190°C. Line two cookie sheets with parchment paper.

2 Put the butter and sugar into a bowl and mix well with a wooden spoon, then beat in the egg yolk and orange extract. Sift together the flour and salt into the mixture, add the chocolate chips, and stir until thoroughly combined.

3 For the coating, mix together the sugar and cinnamon in a shallow dish. Scoop out tablespoons of the cookie dough, roll them into balls, then roll them in the cinnamon mixture to coat. Flatten the cookies slightly with your fingers and put them on the prepared cookie sheets, spaced well apart.

4 Bake in the preheated oven for 12–15 minutes. Let cool on the cookie sheets for 5–10 minutes, then, using a metal spatula, carefully transfer to wire racks to cool completely.

Cranberry & Coconut
COOKIES

Makes about 30

- 1 cup butter, softened
- scant ¾ cup superfine sugar
- 1 egg yolk, lightly beaten
- 2 tsp vanilla extract
- 2½ cups all-purpose flour
- pinch of salt
- ½ cup unsweetened dried coconut
- ½ cup dried cranberries

1 Preheat the oven to 375°F/190°C. Line two cookie sheets with parchment paper.

2 Put the butter and sugar into a bowl and mix well with a wooden spoon, then beat in the egg yolk and vanilla extract. Sift together the flour and salt into the mixture, add the coconut and cranberries, and stir until thoroughly combined. Scoop up tablespoons of the dough and place in mounds on the prepared cookie sheets, spaced well apart.

3 Bake in the preheated oven for 12–15 minutes, until golden brown. Let cool on the cookie sheets for 5–10 minutes, then, using a metal spatula, carefully transfer to wire racks to cool completely.

Cookie
CANDY CANES

Makes 40

- 3 cups all-purpose flour, plus extra for dusting
- 1 tsp baking soda
- scant ½ cup butter, softened, plus extra for greasing
- heaping ¾ cup brown sugar
- 1 egg, beaten
- 1 tsp vanilla extract
- 4 tbsp light corn syrup

To decorate

- 4 cups confectioners' sugar
- generous ½ cup lemon juice
- glycerin-based red food coloring

1 Preheat the oven to 350°F/180°C. Grease three cookie sheets.

2 Sift the flour and baking soda together into a bowl. Add the butter and rub into the flour until the mixture resembles fine breadcrumbs, then stir in the brown sugar. In another bowl, beat together the egg, vanilla extract, and light corn syrup with a fork. Pour this mixture into the flour blend and stir to make a smooth dough, kneading lightly with your hands.

3 Roll the dough out on a lightly floured surface to about ¼ inch/5 mm thick and cut into shapes using a candy cane-shape cutter. Transfer the cookies to the prepared cookie sheets. Bake in the preheated oven for 10 minutes, until golden brown. Remove the cookies from the oven and let cool for 5 minutes, before transferring, using a spatula, to a wire rack to cool completely.

4 Once the cookies are cool, combine 2½ cups of the confectioners' sugar and 5 tablespoons of lemon juice until smooth. Spoon the mixture into a pastry bag fitted with a very fine tip and pipe the icing around the edge of the cookies. Empty any remaining icing into a small bowl, color it with the red food coloring, and cover with plastic wrap.

5 Combine the remaining confectioners' sugar and remaining lemon juice until smooth and runny. Spoon this into the center of each cookie and encourage it to the piped edge to flood each cookie. Let set overnight.

6 Spoon the red icing into a pastry bag fitted with a very fine tip and pipe stripes, dots, and swirls over the dry iced cookies.

Cinnamon & Caramel
COOKIES

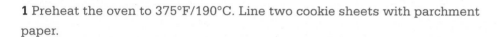

Makes about 25

- 1 cup butter, softened
- scant ¾ cup superfine sugar
- 1 egg yolk, lightly beaten
- 1 tsp vanilla extract
- 2½ cups all-purpose flour
- 1 tsp ground cinnamon
- ½ tsp allspice
- pinch of salt
- 25–30 hard caramel candies

1 Preheat the oven to 375°F/190°C. Line two cookie sheets with parchment paper.

2 Put the butter and sugar into a bowl and mix well with a wooden spoon, then beat in the egg yolk and vanilla extract. Sift together the flour, cinnamon, allspice, and salt into the mixture and stir until thoroughly combined.

3 Scoop up tablespoons of the mixture, shape into balls, and put on the prepared cookie sheets, spaced well apart. Bake in the preheated oven for 8 minutes. Place a caramel candy on top of each cookie, return to the oven, and bake for 6–7 minutes more.

4 Remove from the oven and let cool on the cookie sheets for 5–10 minutes. Using a metal spatula, carefully transfer the cookies to wire racks to cool completely.

Apple &
SPICE COOKIES

Makes about 30

- 1 cup butter, softened
- scant ¾ cup superfine sugar
- 1 egg yolk, lightly beaten
- 2 tsp apple juice
- 2½ cups all-purpose flour
- ½ tsp ground cinnamon
- ½ tsp apple pie spice
- pinch of salt
- scant 1 cup finely chopped plumped dried apple

Apple filling
- 1 tbsp superfine sugar
- 1 tbsp vanilla pudding mix
- ½ cup milk
- 5 tbsp applesauce

1 Put the butter and sugar into a bowl and mix well with a wooden spoon, then beat in the egg yolk and apple juice. Sift together the flour, cinnamon, apple pie spice, and salt into the mixture, add the dried apple, and stir until thoroughly combined. Halve the dough, shape into balls, wrap in plastic wrap, and chill in the refrigerator for 30–60 minutes.

2 Preheat the oven to 375°F/190°C. Line two cookie sheets with parchment paper.

3 Unwrap the dough and roll out between two sheets of parchment paper. Stamp out cookies with a 2-inch/5-cm square cutter and put them on the prepared cookie sheets, spaced well apart. Bake in the preheated oven for 10–15 minutes, until light golden brown. Let cool on the cookie sheets for 5–10 minutes, then, using a metal spatula, carefully transfer to wire racks to cool completely.

4 To make the filling, combine the sugar, pudding mix, and milk in a saucepan and bring to a boil, stirring continuously. Cook, stirring continuously, until thickened, then remove the saucepan from the heat and stir in the applesauce. Cover the surface with plastic wrap and let cool.

5 Spread the filling over half of the cookies and top with the remainder.

Christmas
BELLS

Makes about 30
- 1 cup butter, softened
- scant ¾ cup superfine sugar
- finely grated rind of 1 lemon
- 1 egg yolk, lightly beaten
- 2½ cups all-purpose flour
- ½ tsp ground cinnamon
- pinch of salt
- heaping ½ cup semisweet chocolate chips

To decorate
- 2 tbsp lightly beaten egg white
- 2 tbsp lemon juice
- 2 cups confectioners' sugar
- 30 edible silver balls
- food coloring pens

1 Put the butter, superfine sugar, and lemon rind into a bowl and mix well with a wooden spoon, then beat in the egg yolk. Sift together the flour, cinnamon, and salt into the mixture, add the chocolate chips, and stir until thoroughly combined. Halve the dough, shape into balls, wrap in plastic wrap, and chill in the refrigerator for 30–60 minutes.

2 Preheat the oven to 375°F/190°C. Line two cookie sheets with parchment paper.

3 Unwrap the dough and roll out between two sheets of parchment paper. Stamp out cookies with a 2-inch/5-cm bell-shape cutter and put them on the prepared cookie sheets, spaced well apart.

4 Bake in the preheated oven for 10–15 minutes, until light golden brown. Let cool on the cookie sheets for 5–10 minutes, then, using a metal spatula, carefully transfer to wire racks to cool completely.

5 Combine the egg white and lemon juice in a bowl, then gradually beat in the confectioners' sugar until smooth. With the cookies still on the racks, spread the icing over them. Place a silver ball on the clapper shape at the bottom of the cookie and let set completely. When the icing is dry, use the food coloring pens to draw patterns on the cookies.

Date & Lemon
SPIRALS

Makes about 30

- 1 cup butter, softened
- scant 1 cup superfine sugar
- 1 egg yolk, lightly beaten
- 1 tsp lemon extract
- 2½ cups all-purpose flour
- pinch of salt
- 1⅔ cups pitted and finely chopped dried dates
- 2 tbsp lemon blossom honey
- 5 tbsp lemon juice
- 1 tbsp finely grated lemon rind
- 1 tsp ground cinnamon

1 Put the butter and scant ¾ cup of the sugar into a bowl and mix well with a wooden spoon, then beat in the egg yolk and lemon extract. Sift together the flour and salt into the mixture and stir until thoroughly combined. Shape the dough into a ball, wrap in plastic wrap, and chill in the refrigerator for 30–60 minutes.

2 Meanwhile, put the dates, honey, lemon juice, and lemon rind in a saucepan and stir in ½ cup of water. Bring to a boil, stirring continuously, then lower the heat and simmer gently, stirring occasionally, for 5 minutes. Remove from the heat and let cool, then chill in the refrigerator for 15 minutes.

3 Combine the cinnamon and remaining sugar in a bowl. Unwrap the dough and roll out between two sheets of parchment paper into a 12-inch/30-cm square. Sprinkle the cinnamon-and-sugar mixture over the dough and roll lightly with the rolling pin. Spread the date mixture evenly over the dough, then roll up like a jelly roll. Wrap in plastic wrap and chill in the refrigerator for 30 minutes.

4 Preheat the oven to 375°F/190°C. Line two cookie sheets with parchment paper. Unwrap the roll and cut into thin slices with a sharp serrated knife. Put them on the prepared cookie sheets, spaced well apart. Bake in the preheated oven for 12–15 minutes.

Cinnamon
STARS

Makes 20

- 2 egg whites
- 1½ cups confectioners' sugar, plus extra for dusting
- 2¼ cups roasted ground hazelnuts
- 1 tbsp ground cinnamon

1 Whisk the egg whites in a clean dry bowl until stiff. Stir in the sugar until thoroughly combined, then continue to whisk until thick and glossy.

2 Remove one-sixth of this mixture and set aside. Then fold in the hazelnuts and cinnamon into the remaining mixture to make a very stiff dough. Chill in the refrigerator for about 1 hour.

3 Preheat the oven to 275°F/140°C. Line two cookie sheets with parchment paper. Roll out the dough to ½ inch/1 cm thick on a counter generously dusted with confectioners' sugar.

4 Cut the dough into shapes using a 2-inch/5-cm star-shape cutter, dusting with confectioners' sugar in between to prevent it from sticking. Reroll as necessary until all the mixture is used up.

5 Place the cookies on the prepared cookie sheets, spaced well apart, and spread the top of each star with the reserved egg white icing.

6 Bake in the preheated oven for 25 minutes, until the cookies are still white and crisp on top but slightly soft and moist underneath. Turn off the oven and open the oven door to release the heat and dry out the cookies in the oven for 10 more minutes. Transfer to wire racks to cool.

Blueberry, Cranberry & Cinnamon
COOKIES

Makes about 30
- 1 cup butter, softened
- scant ¾ cup superfine sugar
- 1 egg yolk, lightly beaten
- 2 tsp vanilla extract
- 2½ cups all-purpose flour
- 1 tsp ground cinnamon
- pinch of salt
- ½ cup dried blueberries
- ½ cup dried cranberries
- ½ cup pine nuts, chopped

1 Preheat the oven to 375°F/190°C. Line two cookie sheets with parchment paper.

2 Put the butter and sugar into a bowl and mix well with a wooden spoon, then beat in the egg yolk and vanilla extract. Sift together the flour, cinnamon, and salt into the mixture, add the blueberries and cranberries, and stir until thoroughly combined.

3 Spread out the pine nuts in a shallow dish. Scoop up tablespoons of the mixture and roll them into balls. Roll the balls in the pine nuts to coat, then place on the prepared cookie sheets, spaced well apart, and flatten slightly.

4 Bake in the preheated oven for 10–15 minutes. Let cool on the cookie sheets for 5–10 minutes, then, using a metal spatula, carefully transfer the cookies to wire racks to cool completely.

Apple Suns &
PEAR STARS

Makes about 30

- 1 cup butter, softened
- scant ¾ cup superfine sugar
- 1 egg yolk, lightly beaten
- 2½ cups all-purpose flour
- pinch of salt
- ½ tsp apple pie spice
- ½ cup finely chopped plumped dried apple
- ½ tsp ground ginger
- ½ cup finely chopped plumped dried pear
- ¼ cup sliced almonds
- 1 egg white, lightly beaten
- raw brown sugar, for sprinkling

1 Put the butter and superfine sugar into a bowl and mix well with a wooden spoon, then beat in the egg yolk. Sift together the flour and salt into the mixture and stir until thoroughly combined. Transfer half of the dough to another bowl.

2 Add the apple pie spice and dried apple to one bowl and mix well. Shape into a ball, wrap in plastic wrap, and chill in the refrigerator for 30–60 minutes. Add the ginger and dried pear to the other bowl and mix well. Shape into a ball, wrap in plastic wrap, and chill in the refrigerator for 30–60 minutes.

3 Preheat the oven to 375°F/190°C. Line two cookie sheets with parchment paper.

4 Unwrap the apple-flavored dough and roll out between two sheets of parchment paper to about ⅛ inch/3 mm thick. Stamp out cookies with a sun-shape cutter and put them on a prepared cookie sheet. Repeat with the pear-flavored dough and stamp out cookies with a star-shape cutter. Put them on the other prepared cookie sheet.

5 Bake in the preheated oven for 5 minutes, then remove the star-shape cookies from the oven and sprinkle with the sliced almonds. Return to the oven and bake for 5–10 minutes. Remove the cookies from the oven but do not turn off the heat. Brush the apple suns with a little egg white and sprinkle with the raw brown sugar. Return to the oven for 2–3 minutes. Let all the cookies cool for 5–10 minutes, then carefully transfer them to wire racks to cool completely.

White Chocolate &
PLUM COOKIES

Makes about 30

- 1 cup butter, softened
- scant ¾ cup superfine sugar
- 1 egg yolk, lightly beaten
- 2 tsp vanilla extract
- 2 cups all-purpose flour
- ½ cup unsweetened cocoa
- pinch of salt
- 3½ oz/100 g white chocolate, chopped

To decorate

- 2 oz/55 g white chocolate, broken into pieces
- 15 plumped dried plums, halved

1 Put the butter and sugar into a bowl and mix well with a wooden spoon, then beat in the egg yolk and vanilla extract. Sift together the flour, unsweetened cocoa, and salt into the mixture and stir until thoroughly combined. Halve the dough, shape into balls, wrap in plastic wrap, and chill in the refrigerator for 30–60 minutes.

2 Preheat the oven to 375°F/190°C. Line two cookie sheets with parchment paper. Unwrap a ball of dough and roll out between two sheets of parchment paper to about ⅛ inch/3 mm thick. Stamp out 15 cookies with a plain 2-inch/5-cm cutter and put them on the prepared cookie sheets, spaced well apart. Divide the chopped chocolate among the cookies. Roll out the remaining dough between two sheets of parchment paper and stamp out cookies with a 2½–2¾-inch/6–7-cm cutter. Place them on top of the first cookies and press the edges together to seal.

3 Bake in the preheated oven for 10–15 minutes, until firm. Let cool for 5–10 minutes, then carefully transfer the cookies to wire racks to cool completely. To decorate, melt the chocolate in a heatproof bowl set over a saucepan of gently simmering water. Remove from the heat and let cool slightly. With the cookies still on the racks, dip the cut sides of the plums into the melted chocolate and stick them in the middle of the cookies. Spoon the remaining melted chocolate over them and let set.

Walnut & Fig
PINWHEELS

Makes about 30
- 1 cup butter, softened
- 1 cup superfine sugar
- 1 egg yolk, lightly beaten
- 2 cups all-purpose flour
- pinch of salt
- ½ cup ground walnuts
- 1⅔ cups dried figs, finely chopped
- 5 tbsp freshly brewed mint tea
- 2 tsp finely chopped fresh mint

1 Put the butter and scant ¾ cup of the sugar into a bowl and mix well with a wooden spoon, then beat in the egg yolk. Sift together the flour and salt into the mixture, add the ground walnuts, and stir until thoroughly combined. Shape the dough into a ball, wrap in plastic wrap, and chill in the refrigerator for 30–60 minutes.

2 Meanwhile, put the remaining sugar into a saucepan and stir in ½ cup of water, then add the figs, mint tea, and chopped mint. Bring to a boil, stirring continuously, until the sugar has dissolved, then lower the heat and simmer gently, stirring occasionally, for 5 minutes. Remove the saucepan from the heat and let cool.

3 Unwrap the dough and roll out between two sheets of parchment paper into a 12-inch/30-cm square. Spread the fig filling evenly over the dough, then roll up like a jelly roll. Wrap in plastic wrap and chill in the refrigerator for 30 minutes.

4 Preheat the oven to 375°F/190°C. Line two cookie sheets with parchment paper.

5 Unwrap the roll and cut into thin slices with a sharp serrated knife. Put the slices on the prepared cookie sheets, spaced well apart. Bake in the preheated oven for 10–15 minutes, until golden brown. Let cool on the cookie sheets for 5–10 minutes, then, using a metal spatula, transfer to wire racks to cool completely.

Christmas
TREE COOKIES

Makes 12

- heaping 1 cup all-purpose flour, plus extra for dusting
- 1 tsp ground cinnamon
- ½ tsp ground nutmeg
- ½ tsp ground ginger
- 5 tbsp unsalted butter, diced, plus extra for greasing
- 3 tbsp honey

Decorating
- white icing (optional)
- edible colored balls (optional)

1 Sift the flour and spices into a bowl and rub in the butter until the mixture resembles breadcrumbs. Add the honey and mix together well to form a soft dough. Wrap the dough in plastic wrap and chill in the refrigerator for 30 minutes.

2 Meanwhile, preheat the oven to 350°F/180°C and grease two cookie sheets. Divide the dough in half. Roll out one piece of dough on a floured counter to about ¼ inch/5 mm thick. Cut out tree shapes using a cutter or cardboard template. Repeat with the remaining piece of dough.

3 Put the cookies on the prepared cookie sheets and, using a toothpick, make a hole through the top of each cookie large enough to thread a ribbon through. Chill in the refrigerator for 15 minutes.

4 Bake in the preheated oven for 10 to 12 minutes, until golden. Let cool on the cookie sheets for 5 minutes, then transfer to a wire rack to cool completely. Decorate the trees with white icing and colored balls, or simply leave them plain, then thread a length of ribbon through each hole and knot. Hang from the Christmas tree.

Stained-glass Window
COOKIES

Makes about 25

- 2¾ cups all-purpose flour, plus extra for dusting
- pinch of salt
- 1 tsp baking soda
- scant ½ cup unsalted butter, diced
- scant 1 cup superfine sugar
- 1 extra large egg
- 1 tsp vanilla extract
- 4 tbsp light corn syrup
- 9 oz/250 g mixed colored hard fruit candies

1 Sift the flour, salt, and baking soda into a large bowl, add the butter, and rub it in until the mixture resembles breadcrumbs. Stir in the sugar. Place the egg, vanilla extract, and corn syrup in a separate bowl and whisk together. Pour the egg into the flour mixture and mix to form a smooth dough. Wrap in plastic wrap and chill in the refrigerator for 30 minutes.

2 Preheat the oven to 350°F/180°C. Line two large cookie sheets with parchment paper. Roll the dough out on a floured work surface to ¼ inch/5 mm thick. Use a variety of floured cookie cutters to cut out the cookies. Transfer them to the cookie sheets and cut out shapes from the center of the cookies. Using a skewer, make a hole in the top of each cookie.

3 Lightly crush the candies by tapping them with a rolling pin. Unwrap and sort into separate bowls by color. Fill the holes in the centers of the cookies with the crushed candies.

4 Bake in the preheated oven for 10–12 minutes, or until the candies are melted. Make sure the holes are still there, and pierce again if necessary. Let cool on the cookie sheets until the centers have hardened. When cold, thread thin ribbon through the holes to hang up the cookies.

Spiced
FRUIT COOKIES

Makes about 30

- 1 cup butter, softened
- scant 3¾ cup superfine sugar
- 1 egg yolk, lightly beaten
- 2½ cups all-purpose flour
- ½ tsp apple pie spice
- pinch of salt
- ¼ cup chopped plumped dried apple
- ¼ cup chopped plumped dried pear
- ¼ cup chopped plumped dried plum
- grated rind of 1 orange

1 Put the butter and sugar into a bowl and mix well with a wooden spoon, then beat in the egg yolk. Sift together the flour, apple pie spice, and salt into the mixture, add the apple, pear, plum, and orange rind, and stir until thoroughly combined. Shape the dough into a log, wrap in plastic wrap, and chill in the refrigerator for 30–60 minutes.

2 Preheat the oven to 375°F/190°C. Line two cookie sheets with parchment paper.

3 Unwrap the log and cut it into ¼-inch/5-mm thick slices with a sharp serrated knife. Put them on the prepared cookie sheets, spaced well apart.

4 Bake in the preheated oven for 10–15 minutes, until golden brown. Let cool on the cookie sheets for 5–10 minutes, then, using a metal spatula, carefully transfer the cookies to wire racks to cool completely.

GINGERSNAPS

Makes 30
- 2½ cups self-rising flour
- pinch of salt
- 1 cup superfine sugar
- 1 tbsp ground ginger
- 1 tsp baking soda
- ½ cup butter, plus extra for greasing
- ¼ cup light corn syrup
- 1 egg, lightly beaten
- 1 tsp grated orange rind

1 Preheat the oven to 325°F/160°C. Grease two cookie sheets.

2 Sift together the flour, salt, sugar, ground ginger, and baking soda into a large mixing bowl.

3 Heat the butter and corn syrup together in a saucepan over very low heat until the butter has melted. Let the butter mixture cool slightly, then pour it onto the dry ingredients. Add the egg and orange rind and mix together thoroughly.

4 Using your hands, carefully shape the dough into 30 even-size balls. Place the balls on the prepared cookie sheets, spaced well apart, and flatten slightly with your fingers.

5 Bake in the preheated oven for 15–20 minutes. Carefully transfer the cookies to a wire rack to cool and crisp.

Christmas Tree
DECORATIONS

Makes 20–25

- 1 cup butter, softened
- scant ¾ cup superfine sugar
- 1 egg yolk, lightly beaten
- 2 tsp vanilla extract
- 2½ cups all-purpose flour
- pinch of salt
- 1 egg white, lightly beaten
- 2 tbsp colored sprinkles
- 14 oz/400 g mixed colored hard fruit candies

1 Put the butter and sugar into a bowl and mix, then beat in the egg yolk and vanilla extract. Sift together the flour and salt into the mixture and stir until thoroughly combined. Halve the dough, shape into balls, wrap in plastic wrap, and chill in the refrigerator for 30–60 minutes.

2 Preheat the oven to 375°F/190°C. Line two cookie sheets with parchment paper.

3 Unwrap the dough and roll out between two sheets of parchment paper. Stamp out cookies with Christmas-themed cutters and put them on the prepared cookie sheets, spaced well apart. Using the end of a large plain piping tip, stamp out rounds from each shape and remove them. Make a small hole in the top of each cookie with a skewer so that they can be threaded with ribbon. Brush with egg white and decorate with the sprinkles. Bake in the preheated oven for 7 minutes.

4 Meanwhile, lightly crush the candies by tapping them with a rolling pin. Unwrap and sort into separate bowls by color. Remove the cookies from the oven and fill the holes with the crushed candies. Return to the oven and bake for an additional 5–8 minutes, until the cookies are light golden brown and the candies have melted and filled the holes. If the holes for hanging the cookies have closed up, pierce them again with the skewer while the cookies are still warm. If there are any gaps in the cookies, gently spread the melted candies with the skewer to fill. Let cool completely on the cookie sheets. Thread thin ribbon through and hang.

Holly
LEAF COOKIES

Makes 30
- 4 tbsp butter, softened, plus extra for greasing
- scant ½ cup superfine sugar
- 1 egg yolk
- ⅛ tsp almond extract
- 1 cup all-purpose flour, plus extra for dusting
- 2 tsp milk
- 3 oz/85 g mixed colored hard fruit candies

1 Beat the butter and sugar together in a bowl until light and fluffy. Beat in the egg yolk and almond extract until smooth and then sift in the flour and add the milk to produce a soft dough. Cover with plastic wrap and chill in the refrigerator for 30 minutes.

2 Preheat the oven to 350°F/180°C. Grease two cookie sheets. Crush the candies in their wrappers with a rolling pin. Roll out the chilled dough on a lightly floured counter to ¼ inch/5 mm thick.

3 Use a large holly leaf-shape cutter to cut out shapes from the dough and then use a smaller holly shape cutter to cut out and remove the middle of each larger holly shape.

4 Place all the holly shapes on the prepared cookie sheets. Using a toothpick, cut a small hole out of the top of each cookie so they can be threaded with ribbon. Reknead and reroll the dough trimmings and cut out leaves until all the dough is used up.

5 Divide the crushed hard candy pieces evenly to fill the holes in the middle of the cookies. Bake in the preheated oven for 8–10 minutes, until the cookies are just turning golden around the edges.

6 When completely cool, transfer the cookies, using a metal spatula, to a wire rack. Thread thin ribbons through the holes and hang from the branches of the Christmas tree.

Peach, Pear &
PLUM COOKIES

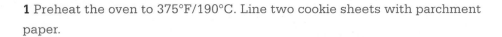

Makes about 30

- 1 cup butter, softened
- scant ¾ cup superfine sugar
- 1 egg yolk, lightly beaten
- 2 tsp almond extract
- 2½ cups all-purpose flour
- pinch of salt
- ½ cup finely chopped plumped dried peach
- ½ cup finely chopped plumped dried pear
- 4 tbsp plum jelly

1 Preheat the oven to 375°F/190°C. Line two cookie sheets with parchment paper.

2 Put the butter and sugar into a bowl and mix well with a wooden spoon, then beat in the egg yolk and almond extract. Sift together the flour and salt into the mixture, add the dried fruit, and stir until thoroughly combined.

3 Scoop up tablespoons of the mixture, roll them into balls, and put on the prepared cookie sheets, spaced well apart. Make a hollow in the center of each with the dampened handle of a wooden spoon. Fill the hollows with plum jelly.

4 Bake in the preheated oven for 12–15 minutes, until light golden brown. Let cool on the cookie sheets for 5–10 minutes, then, using a metal spatula, carefully transfer to wire racks to cool completely.

Iced STARS

Makes 30

- 1 cup butter, softened
- ¾ cup superfine sugar
- 1 egg yolk, lightly beaten
- ½ tsp vanilla extract
- 2 cups all-purpose flour
- pinch of salt

To decorate

- 1¾ cups confectioners' sugar
- 1–2 tbsp warm water
- food colorings
- edible silver and gold balls
- colored sprinkles
- edible sugar stars, hearts, and flowers
- dry unsweetened coconut

1 Place the butter and superfine sugar in a large bowl and beat together until light and fluffy, then beat in the egg yolk and vanilla extract. Sift together the flour and salt into the mixture and stir until thoroughly combined. Halve the dough, shape into balls, wrap in plastic wrap, and chill in the refrigerator for 30–60 minutes.

2 Preheat the oven to 375°F/190°C. Line two large cookie sheets with parchment paper.

3 Unwrap the dough and roll out between two sheets of parchment paper to about ⅛ inch/3 mm thick. Cut out cookies with a star-shape cutter and place them on the prepared cookie sheets, spaced well apart. Bake in the preheated oven for 10–15 minutes, or until light golden brown. Let cool on the cookie sheets for 5–10 minutes, then transfer to wire racks to cool completely.

4 To decorate, sift the confectioners' sugar into a bowl and stir in enough warm water until it is the consistency of thick cream. Divide the icing among 3–4 bowls and add a few drops of your chosen food colorings to each. Leave the cookies on the racks and spread the different colored icings over them to the edges. Arrange colored balls on top and/or sprinkle with colored sprinkles and sugar shapes. If you like, color dry unsweetened coconut with food coloring in a contrasting color and sprinkle over the cookies. Let set.

Christmas
GIFT COOKIES

Makes about 30
- 1 cup butter, softened
- ¾ cup superfine sugar
- 1 egg yolk, lightly beaten
- 2 tsp orange juice or orange liqueur
- finely grated rind of 1 orange
- 2 cups all-purpose flour
- pinch of salt

Decorating
- 1 egg white
- 2 cups confectioners' sugar
- few drops each of 2 food colorings
- edible silver balls

1 Place the butter and superfine sugar in a large bowl and beat together until light and fluffy, then beat in the egg yolk, orange juice, and grated rind. Sift together the flour and salt into the mixture and stir until combined. Halve the dough, shape into balls, wrap in plastic wrap, and chill in the refrigerator for 30–60 minutes.

2 Preheat the oven to 375°F/190°C. Line two large cookie sheets with parchment paper. Unwrap the dough and roll out to ⅛ inch/3 mm thick. Cut out appropriate shapes, such as stars, with cookie cutters and place them on the cookie sheets, spaced well apart. Bake in the preheated oven for 10–15 minutes, or until light golden brown.

3 Let cool on the cookie sheets for 5–10 minutes, then transfer the cookies to wire racks to cool completely.

4 Leave the cookies on the racks. Place the egg white and confectioners' sugar in a bowl and beat until smooth, adding a little water, if necessary. Transfer half of the icing to another bowl and color each bowl with a different color. Place both icings in pastry bags with fine tips and use to decorate the cookies and write the initials of the person who will receive the cookies as a gift. Finish with silver balls and let set.

Cinnamon &
ORANGE WAFERS

Makes about 30

- 1 cup butter, softened
- 1 cup superfine sugar
- finely grated rind of 1 orange
- 1 egg yolk, lightly beaten
- 4 tsp orange juice
- 2 cups all-purpose flour
- pinch of salt
- 2 tsp ground cinnamon

1 Place the butter, ¾ cup of the sugar, and the orange rind in a large bowl and beat together until light and fluffy, then beat in the egg yolk and 2 teaspoons of the orange juice. Sift together the flour and salt into the mixture and stir until thoroughly combined. Shape the dough into a ball, wrap in plastic wrap, and chill for 30–60 minutes.

2 Unwrap the dough and roll out between two sheets of parchment paper into a 12-inch/30-cm square. Brush with the remaining orange juice and sprinkle with the remaining sugar and cinnamon. Lightly roll with the rolling pin. Roll up the dough like a jelly roll. Wrap in plastic wrap and chill for 30 minutes.

3 Preheat the oven to 375°F/190°C. Line two large cookie sheets with parchment paper.

4 Unwrap the dough and cut into thin slices, then place on the prepared cookie sheets, spaced well apart. Bake in the preheated oven for 10–12 minutes. Let cool for 5–10 minutes, then transfer to wire racks to cool completely.

Christmas
ANGELS

Makes about 25

- 1 cup butter, softened
- scant ¾ cup superfine sugar
- 1 egg yolk, lightly beaten
- 2 tsp passion fruit pulp
- 2½ cups all-purpose flour
- pinch of salt
- ⅔ cup dry unsweetened coconut

To decorate

- 1½ cups confectioners' sugar
- 1–1½ tbsp passion fruit pulp
- edible silver glitter, for sprinkling

1 Put the butter and superfine sugar into a bowl and mix well with a wooden spoon, then beat in the egg yolk and passion fruit pulp. Sift together the flour and salt into the mixture, add the coconut, and stir until thoroughly combined. Halve the dough, shape into balls, wrap in plastic wrap, and chill in the refrigerator for 30–60 minutes.

2 Preheat the oven to 375°F/190°C. Line two cookie sheets with parchment paper.

3 Unwrap the dough and roll out between two sheets of parchment paper. Stamp out cookies with a 2¾-inch/7-cm angel-shape cutter and put them on the prepared cookie sheets, spaced well apart.

4 Bake in the preheated oven for 10–15 minutes, until light golden brown. Let cool on the cookie sheets for 5–10 minutes, then, using a metal spatula, carefully transfer to wire racks to cool completely.

5 Sift the confectioners' sugar into a bowl and stir in the passion fruit pulp until the icing has the consistency of thick cream. With the cookies still on the racks, spread the icing over them. Sprinkle with the edible glitter and let set.

Chocolate, Date & Pecan
PINWHEELS

Makes about 30
- 1 cup butter, softened
- 1 cup superfine sugar
- 1 egg yolk, lightly beaten
- 1⅔ cups all-purpose flour
- ½ cup unsweetened cocoa
- pinch of salt
- ⅔ cup pecans, finely ground
- 1⅔ cups coarsely chopped, pitted dried dates
- finely grated rind of 1 orange
- ¾ cup orange flower water

1 Place the butter and ¾ cup of the sugar in a large bowl and beat together until light and fluffy, then beat in the egg yolk. Sift together the flour, cocoa, and salt into the mixture, add the nuts, and stir until combined. Halve the dough, shape into balls, wrap in plastic wrap, and chill in the refrigerator for 30–60 minutes.

2 Meanwhile, place the dates, orange rind, orange flower water, and remaining sugar into a saucepan and cook over low heat, stirring, until the sugar has dissolved. Bring to a boil, then reduce the heat and simmer, for 5 minutes. Pour the mixture into a bowl, cool, then chill.

3 Unwrap the dough and roll out between two sheets of parchment paper to rectangles ¼ inch/5 mm thick. Spread the filling over the rectangles and roll up like a jelly roll. Wrap in the paper and chill in the refrigerator for 30 minutes. Preheat the oven to 375°F/190°C. Line two large cookie sheets with parchment paper. Unwrap the rolls, cut into ½-inch/1-cm slices and place them on the prepared cookie sheets.

4 Bake in the preheated oven for 15–20 minutes, or until golden brown. Let cool on the prepared cookie sheets for 5–10 minutes, then transfer the cookies to wire racks to cool completely.

German
LEBKUCHEN

....

Makes 60

- 3 eggs
- 1 cup superfine sugar
- heaping ⅓ cup all-purpose flour
- 2 tsp unsweetened cocoa
- 1 tsp ground cinnamon
- ½ tsp ground cardamom
- ¼ tsp ground cloves
- ¼ tsp ground nutmeg
- 2 cups ground almonds
- ⅓ cup candied peel, finely chopped

To decorate
- 4 oz/115 g semisweet chocolate, broken into pieces
- 4 oz/115 g white chocolate, broken into pieces
- sugar crystals

1 Preheat the oven to 350°F/180°C. Line several large cookie sheets with parchment paper. Place the eggs and sugar in a heatproof bowl set over a saucepan of gently simmering water and whisk until thick and foamy. Remove the bowl from the pan and continue to whisk for 2 minutes.

2 Sift the flour, cocoa, cinnamon, cardamom, cloves, and nutmeg into the bowl and stir in with the ground almonds and candied peel. Drop heaping teaspoonfuls of the mixture onto the prepared cookie sheets, spreading them gently into smooth mounds.

3 Bake in the preheated oven for 15–20 minutes, or until light brown and slightly soft to the touch. Let cool on the cookie sheets for 10 minutes, then transfer the cookies to wire racks to cool completely.

4 Place the semisweet and white chocolates in two separate heatproof bowls, set the bowls over two pans of gently simmering water, and heat until melted. Dip half of the cookies in the melted semisweet chocolate and half in the white chocolate. Sprinkle with sugar crystals and let set.

Spicy Cinnamon
DRIZZLES

Makes about 25

- scant 1 cup butter, softened
- 2 tbsp molasses
- scant ¾ cup superfine sugar
- 1 egg yolk, lightly beaten
- 2½ cups all-purpose flour
- 1 tsp ground cinnamon
- ½ tsp ground nutmeg
- ½ tsp ground cloves
- pinch of salt
- 2 tbsp chopped walnuts

To decorate

- 1 cup confectioners' sugar
- 1 tbsp hot water
- a few drops of yellow food coloring
- a few drops of pink food coloring

1 Put the butter, molasses, and superfine sugar into a bowl and mix well with a wooden spoon, then beat in the egg yolk. Sift together the flour, cinnamon, nutmeg, cloves, and salt into the mixture, add the walnuts, and stir until thoroughly combined. Halve the dough, shape into balls, wrap in plastic wrap, and chill in the refrigerator for 30–60 minutes.

2 Preheat the oven to 375°F/190°C. Line two cookie sheets with parchment paper.

3 Unwrap the dough and roll out between two sheets of parchment paper to about ¼ inch/5 mm thick. Stamp out cookies with a 2½-inch/6-cm fluted cutter and put them on the prepared cookie sheets.

4 Bake in the preheated oven for 10–15 minutes, until firm. Let cool on the cookie sheets for 5–10 minutes, then, using a metal spatula, carefully transfer the cookies to wire racks to cool completely.

5 To decorate, sift the confectioners' sugar into a bowl, then gradually stir in the hot water until the icing has the consistency of thick cream. Spoon half of the icing into another bowl and stir a few drops of yellow food coloring into one bowl and a few drops of pink food coloring into the other. With the cookies still on the racks, using teaspoons, drizzle the yellow icing over them in one direction and the pink icing over them at right angles. Let set.

Silver
STAR COOKIES

Makes 36
- ½ cup all-purpose flour, plus extra for dusting
- 1 tsp ground cinnamon
- 1 tsp ground ginger
- 6½ tbsp butter, diced
- scant ½ cup light brown sugar
- finely grated rind of 1 orange
- 1 egg, lightly beaten

To decorate
- 1¾ cups confectioners' sugar
- 3–4 tsp cold water
- edible silver cake sprinkles
- edible silver balls

1 Preheat the oven to 350°F/180°C. Line several large cookie sheets with parchment paper.

2 Sift the flour, cinnamon, and ginger into a large bowl. Add the butter and rub it in with your fingertips until the mixture resembles fine breadcrumbs. Stir the brown sugar and orange rind into the mixture, add the egg, and mix together to form a soft dough.

3 Roll the dough out thinly to about ¼ inch/5 mm thick on a lightly floured work surface. Cut out shapes with a 2½-inch/6.5-cm snowflake- or star-shape cutter and place on the prepared cookie sheets.

4 Bake in the preheated oven for 10–15 minutes, or until golden brown. Let cool on the cookie sheets for 2–3 minutes, then transfer the cookies to a wire rack and let cool completely.

5 To make the icing, sift the confectioners' sugar into a large bowl and add enough water to make a smooth icing. Spread a little on each cookie, then decorate with sprinkles and silver balls.

Christmas Stocking COOKIES

Makes 30

- scant ⅓ cup butter, plus extra for greasing
- ¼ cup superfine sugar
- 1 egg, beaten
- finely grated rind and juice of 1 lemon
- 2 cups all-purpose flour, plus extra for dusting

- ¼ cup cornstarch, plus extra for dusting
- ½ tsp baking powder
- 1 tbsp apple pie spice

To decorate
- glycerin-base red and green food coloring

- 9 oz/250 g ready-to-use fondant
- 2½ cups confectioners' sugar
- 1 egg white
- ½ tsp glycerin

1 Beat together the butter and superfine sugar in a bowl with an electric mixer until creamy. Then beat in the egg and lemon rind. Sift together the flour, cornstarch, baking powder, and spice into the batter and stir to combine thoroughly into a soft dough. Wrap in plastic wrap and chill for 30 minutes.

2 Preheat the oven to 350°F/180°C. Grease two cookie sheets. Roll out the dough on a lightly floured counter to ¼ inch/5 mm thick. Using a Christmas stocking-shape cutter, cut out shapes from the dough and place on the prepared cookie sheets. Reknead and reroll the trimmings and cut out shapes until all the dough is used up. Bake in the preheated oven for 15 minutes, until just golden. Let cool for 5 minutes before transferring to a wire rack to cool.

3 Mix the green coloring into 1 oz/25 g of the fondant, adding a little confectioners' sugar, until well blended. Cover to prevent it from drying out. Repeat with remaining fondant and the red food coloring. Roll out the green fondant as thinly as possible on a surface lightly dusted with cornstarch and cut out shapes using a small holly-leaf cutter. Set aside. Roll out the red fondant, again as thinly as possible. Cut out shapes using the Christmas stocking-shape cutter. Stick each stocking to the cookie by using a little lemon juice. Beat together the remaining confectioners' sugar, the egg white, and glycerin for 5 minutes with an electric mixer until stiff and glossy. Slacken the mixture with a little lemon juice to make it thick, but still possible to pipe. Fill a pastry bag, fitted with a small star-shape nozzle, with this icing mixture. Pipe rows of stars to form a furry cuff on each stocking. Stick a holly-leaf shape into the piped icing on each cookie.